Buddhist Teachings on Right Speech: Discourses from Samyutta Nikaya

Bodhi Path Press

GRAPEVINE INDIA

Published by

GRAPEVINE INDIA PUBLISHERS PVT LTD

www.grapevineindia.com

Delhi | Mumbai

email: grapevineindiapublishers@gmail.com

Ordering Information:

Quantity sales: Special discounts are available on quantity

purchases by corporations, associations, and others.

For details, reach out to the publisher.

First published by Grapevine India 2024

KALYANAMITTASUTTA: GOOD FRIENDS

At Savatthi.

Seated to one side, King Pasenadi said to the Buddha,

"Just now, sir, as I was in private retreat this thought came to mind.

'The teaching is well explained by the Buddha. But it's for someone with good friends, companions, and associates, not for someone with bad friends, companions, and associates.'"

"That's so true, great king! That's so true!" said the Buddha. And he repeated the king's statement, adding:

"Great king, this one time I was staying in the land of the Sakyans where they have a town named Townsville.

Then the mendicant Ananda came to me, bowed, sat down to one side, and said:

'Sir, good friends, companions, and associates are half the spiritual life.'

When he had spoken, I said to him:

'Not so, Ananda! Not so, Ananda!

Good friends, companions, and associates are the whole of the spiritual life.

A mendicant with good friends, companions, and associates can expect to develop and cultivate the noble eightfold path.

And how does a mendicant with good friends develop and cultivate the noble eightfold path?

It's when a mendicant develops right view, right thought, right speech, right action, right livelihood, right effort, right mindfulness, and right immersion, which rely on seclusion, fading away, and cessation, and ripen as letting go.

That's how a mendicant with good friends develops and cultivates the noble eightfold path.

And here's another way to understand how good friends are the whole of the spiritual life.

For, by relying on me as a good friend, sentient beings who are liable to rebirth, old age, and death, to sorrow, lamentation, pain, sadness, and distress are freed from all these things.

This is another way to understand how good friends are the whole of the spiritual life.'

So, great king, you should train like this:

'I will have good friends, companions, and associates.'

That's how you should train.

When you have good friends, companions, and associates, you should live supported by one thing:

diligence in skillful qualities.

When you're diligent, supported by diligence, your ladies of the harem,

aristocrat vassals,

troops,

and people of town and country will think:

'The king lives diligently, supported by diligence.

We'd better live diligently, supported by diligence!'

When you're diligent, supported by diligence, then not only you yourself,

but your ladies of the harem, and your treasury and storehouses will be guarded and protected."

That is what the Buddha said. …

"For one who desires a continuous flow

of exceptional wealth,

the astute praise diligence

in making merit.

Being diligent, an astute person

secures both benefits:

the benefit in this life,

and in lives to come.

A wise one, comprehending the meaning,

is said to be astute."

BHIKKHUSUTTA: A MENDICANT

At Savatthi.

"A mendicant understands old age and death, their origin, their cessation, and the practice that leads to their cessation. They understand rebirth …

continued existence …

grasping …

craving …

feeling …

contact …

the six sense fields …

name and form …

consciousness …

They understand choices, their origin, their cessation, and the practice that leads to their cessation.

And what is old age and death?

The old age, decrepitude, broken teeth, grey hair, wrinkly skin, diminished vitality, and failing faculties of the various sentient beings in the various orders of sentient beings.

This is called old age.

The passing away, perishing, disintegration, demise, mortality, death, decease, breaking up of the aggregates, and laying to rest of the corpse of the various sentient beings in the various orders of sentient beings.

This is called death.

Such is old age, and such is death.

This is called old age and death.

Rebirth is the origin of old age and death.

When rebirth ceases, old age and death cease.

The practice that leads to the cessation of old age and death is simply this noble eightfold path,

that is: right view, right thought, right speech, right action, right livelihood, right effort, right mindfulness, and right immersion.

And what is rebirth? …

And what is continued existence? …

And what is grasping? …

And what is craving? …

feeling …

contact …

the six sense fields …

name and form …

consciousness …

And what are choices?

There are three kinds of choices.

Choices by way of body, speech, and mind.

These are called choices.

Ignorance is the origin of choices.

When ignorance ceases, choices cease.

The practice that leads to the cessation of choices is simply this noble eightfold path,

that is: right view, right thought, right speech, right action, right livelihood, right effort, right mindfulness, and right immersion.

A mendicant understands old age and death, their origin, their cessation, and the practice that leads to their cessation. They understand rebirth …

continued existence …

grasping …

craving …

feeling …

contact …

the six sense fields …

name and form ...

consciousness ...

They understand choices,

their origin,

their cessation,

and the practice that leads to their cessation.

Such a mendicant is called 'one accomplished in view', 'one accomplished in vision', 'one who has come to the true teaching', 'one who sees this true teaching', 'one endowed with a trainee's knowledge', 'one who has entered the stream of the teaching', 'a noble one with penetrative wisdom', and 'one who stands pushing open the door of the deathless'."

NANAVATTHUSUTTA: GROUNDS FOR KNOWLEDGE

At Savatthi.

"Mendicants, I will teach forty-four grounds for knowledge.

Listen and pay close attention, I will speak."

"Yes, sir," they replied.

The Buddha said this:

"And what are the forty-four grounds for knowledge?

Knowledge of old age and death, knowledge of the origin of old age and death, knowledge of the cessation of old age and death, and knowledge of the practice that leads to the cessation of old age and death.

Knowledge of rebirth …

Knowledge of continued existence …

Knowledge of grasping …

Knowledge of craving …

Knowledge of feeling …

Knowledge of contact …

Knowledge of the six sense fields …

Knowledge of name and form …

Knowledge of consciousness …

Knowledge of choices, knowledge of the origin of choices, knowledge of the cessation of choices, and knowledge of the practice that leads to the cessation of choices.

These are called the forty-four grounds for knowledge.

And what is old age and death?

The old age, decrepitude, broken teeth, grey hair, wrinkly skin, diminished vitality, and failing faculties of the various sentient beings in the various orders of sentient beings.

This is called old age.

The passing away, perishing, disintegration, demise, mortality, death, decease, breaking up of the aggregates, and laying to rest of the corpse of the various sentient beings in the various orders of sentient beings.

This is called death.

Such is old age, and such is death.

This is called old age and death.

Rebirth is the origin of old age and death.

When rebirth ceases, old age and death cease.

The practice that leads to the cessation of old age and death is simply this noble eightfold path, that is:

right view, right thought, right speech, right action, right livelihood, right effort, right mindfulness, and right immersion.

A noble disciple understands old age and death, their origin, their cessation, and the practice that leads to their cessation. This is their knowledge of the present phenomenon.

With this present phenomenon that is seen, known, immediate, attained, and fathomed, they infer to the past and future.

Whatever ascetics and brahmins in the past directly knew old age and death, their origin, their cessation, and the practice that leads to their cessation, all of them directly knew these things in exactly the same way that I do now.

Whatever ascetics and brahmins in the future will directly know old age and death, their origin, their cessation, and the practice that leads to their cessation, all of them will directly know these things in exactly the same way that I do now.

This is their inferential knowledge.

A noble disciple has purified and cleansed these two knowledges—

knowledge of the present phenomena, and inferential knowledge.

When a noble disciple has done this, they're called 'one accomplished in view', 'one accomplished in vision', 'one who has come to the true teaching', 'one who sees this true teaching', 'one endowed with a trainee's knowledge', 'one who has entered the stream of the teaching', 'a noble one with penetrative wisdom', and 'one who stands pushing open the door of the deathless'.

And what is rebirth? …

And what is continued existence? …

And what is grasping? …

And what is craving? …

And what is feeling? …

And what is contact? …

And what are the six sense fields? …

And what are name and form? …

And what is consciousness? …

And what are choices?

There are three kinds of choices.

Choices by way of body, speech, and mind.

These are called choices.

Ignorance is the origin of choices.

When ignorance ceases, choices cease.

The practice that leads to the cessation of choices is simply this noble eightfold path, that is:

right view, right thought, right speech, right action, right livelihood, right effort, right mindfulness, and right immersion.

A noble disciple understands choices, their origin, their cessation, and the practice that leads to their cessation. This is their knowledge of the present phenomenon.

With this present phenomenon that is seen, known, immediate, attained, and fathomed, they infer to the past and future.

Whatever ascetics and brahmins in the past directly knew choices, their origin, their cessation, and the practice that leads to their cessation, all of them directly knew these things in exactly the same way that I do now.

Whatever ascetics and brahmins in the future will directly know choices, their origin, their cessation, and the practice that leads to their cessation, all of them will directly know these things in exactly the same way that I do now.

This is their inferential knowledge.

A noble disciple has purified and cleansed these two knowledges—

knowledge of the present phenomena, and inferential knowledge.

When a noble disciple has done this, they're called 'one accomplished in view', 'one accomplished in vision', 'one who has come to the true teaching', 'one who sees this true teaching', 'one endowed with a trainee's knowledge', 'one who has entered the stream of the teaching', 'a noble one with penetrative wisdom', and 'one who stands pushing open the door of the deathless'."

UPADANAPARIPAVATTASUTTA: PERSPECTIVES

At Savatthi.

"Mendicants, there are these five grasping aggregates.

What five?

The grasping aggregates of form, feeling, perception, choices, and consciousness.

As long as I didn't truly understand these five grasping aggregates from four perspectives, I didn't announce my supreme perfect awakening in this world with its gods, Maras, and Brahmas, this population with its ascetics and brahmins, its gods and humans.

But when I did truly understand these five grasping aggregates from four perspectives, I announced my supreme perfect awakening in this world with its gods, Maras, and Brahmas, this population with its ascetics and brahmins, its gods and humans.

And how are there four perspectives?

I directly knew form, its origin, its cessation, and the practice that leads to its cessation.

I directly knew feeling …

perception …

choices …

consciousness, its origin, its cessation, and the practice that leads to its cessation.

And what is form?

The four primary elements, and form derived from the four primary elements.

This is called form.

Form originates from food.

When food ceases, form ceases.

The practice that leads to the cessation of form is simply this noble eightfold path, that is:

right view, right thought, right speech, right action, right livelihood, right effort, right mindfulness, and right immersion.

Whatever ascetics and brahmins have directly known form in this way—and its origin, its cessation, and the practice that leads to its cessation—and are practicing for disillusionment, dispassion, and cessation regarding form: they are practicing well.

Those who practice well have a firm footing in this teaching and training.

Those ascetics and brahmins who have directly known form in this way—and its origin, its cessation, and the practice that leads to its cessation—and due to disillusionment, dispassion, and cessation regarding form, are freed by not grasping: they are well freed.

Those who are well freed are consummate ones.

For consummate ones, there is no cycle of rebirths to be found.

And what is feeling?

There are these six classes of feeling:

feeling born of contact through the eye, ear, nose, tongue, body, and mind.

This is called feeling.

Feeling originates from contact.

When contact ceases, feeling ceases.

The practice that leads to the cessation of feelings is simply this noble eightfold path …

And what is perception?

There are these six classes of perception:

perceptions of sights, sounds, smells, tastes, touches, and thoughts.

This is called perception.

Perception originates from contact.

When contact ceases, perception ceases.

The practice that leads to the cessation of perceptions is simply this noble eightfold path …

And what are choices?

There are these six classes of intention:

intention regarding sights, sounds, smells, tastes, touches, and thoughts.

These are called choices.

Choices originate from contact.

When contact ceases, choices cease.

The practice that leads to the cessation of choices is simply this noble eightfold path …

And what is consciousness?

There are these six classes of consciousness:

eye, ear, nose, tongue, body, and mind consciousness.

This is called consciousness.

Consciousness originates from name and form.

When name and form cease, consciousness ceases.

The practice that leads to the cessation of consciousness is simply this noble eightfold path, that is:

right view, right thought, right speech, right action, right livelihood, right effort, right mindfulness, and right immersion.

Whatever ascetics and brahmins have directly known consciousness in this way—and its origin, its cessation, and the practice that leads to its cessation—and are practicing for disillusionment, dispassion, and cessation regarding consciousness: they are practicing well.

Those who practice well have a firm footing in this teaching and training.

Those ascetics and brahmins who have directly known consciousness in this way—and its origin, its cessation, and the practice that leads to its cessation—and due to disillusionment, dispassion, and cessation regarding consciousness, are freed by not grasping: they are well freed.

Those who are well freed are consummate ones.

For consummate ones, there is no cycle of rebirths to be found."

SATTAṬṬHANASUTTA: SEVEN CASES

At Savatthi.

"Mendicants, in this teaching and training a mendicant who is skilled in seven cases and who examines in three ways is called consummate, accomplished, a supreme person.

And how is a mendicant skilled in seven cases?

It's when a mendicant understands form, its origin, its cessation, and the practice that leads to its cessation.

They understand form's gratification, drawback, and escape.

They understand feeling …

perception …

choices …

consciousness, its origin, its cessation, and the practice that leads to its cessation.

They understand consciousness's gratification, drawback, and escape.

And what is form?

The four primary elements, and form derived from the four primary elements.

This is called form.

Form originates from food.

When food ceases, form ceases.

The practice that leads to the cessation of form is simply this noble eightfold path, that is:

right view, right thought, right speech, right action, right livelihood, right effort, right mindfulness, and right immersion.

The pleasure and happiness that arise from form: this is its gratification.

That form is impermanent, suffering, and perishable: this is its drawback.

Removing and giving up desire and greed for form: this is its escape.

Those ascetics and brahmins who have directly known form in this way—and its origin, its cessation, and the practice that leads to its cessation;

its gratification, drawback, and escape—and are practicing for disillusionment, dispassion, and cessation regarding form: they are practicing well.

Those who practice well have a firm footing in this teaching and training.

Those ascetics and brahmins who have directly known form in this way—and its origin, its cessation, and the practice that leads to its cessation;

its gratification, drawback, and escape—and due to disillusionment, dispassion, and cessation regarding form, are freed by not grasping: they are well freed.

Those who are well freed are consummate ones.

For consummate ones, there is no cycle of rebirths to be found.

And what is feeling?

There are these six classes of feeling:

feeling born of eye contact …

feeling born of mind contact.

This is called feeling.

Feeling originates from contact.

When contact ceases, feeling ceases.

The practice that leads to the cessation of feelings is simply this noble eightfold path, that is:

right view, right thought, right speech, right action, right livelihood, right effort, right mindfulness, and right immersion.

The pleasure and happiness that arise from feeling: this is its gratification.

That feeling is impermanent, suffering, and perishable: this is its drawback.

Removing and giving up desire and greed for feeling: this is its escape. …

And what is perception?

There are these six classes of perception:

perceptions of sights, sounds, smells, tastes, touches, and thoughts.

This is called perception.

Perception originates from contact.

When contact ceases, perception ceases.

The practice that leads to the cessation of perceptions is simply this noble eightfold path …

And what are choices?

There are these six classes of intention:

intention regarding sights …

intention regarding thoughts.

These are called choices.

Choices originate from contact.

When contact ceases, choices cease.

The practice that leads to the cessation of choices is simply this noble eightfold path …

And what is consciousness?

There are these six classes of consciousness:

eye, ear, nose, tongue, body, and mind consciousness.

This is called consciousness.

Consciousness originates from name and form.

When name and form cease, consciousness ceases.

The practice that leads to the cessation of consciousness is simply this noble eightfold path, that is:

right view, right thought, right speech, right action, right livelihood, right effort, right mindfulness, and right immersion.

The pleasure and happiness that arise from consciousness: this is its gratification.

That consciousness is impermanent, suffering, and perishable: this is its drawback.

Removing and giving up desire and greed for consciousness: this is its escape.

Those ascetics and brahmins who have directly known consciousness in this way—and its origin, its cessation, and the practice that leads to its cessation;

its gratification, drawback, and escape—and are practicing for disillusionment, dispassion, and cessation regarding consciousness: they are practicing well.

Those who practice well have a firm footing in this teaching and training.

Those ascetics and brahmins who have directly known consciousness in this way—and its origin, its cessation, and the practice that leads to its cessation;

its gratification, drawback, and escape—and due to disillusionment, dispassion, and cessation regarding consciousness, are freed by not grasping: they are well freed.

Those who are well freed are consummate ones.

For consummate ones, there is no cycle of rebirths to be found.

That's how a mendicant is skilled in seven cases.

And how does a mendicant examine in three ways?

It's when a mendicant examines the elements, sense fields, and dependent origination.

That's how a mendicant examines in three ways.

In this teaching and training, a mendicant who is skilled in seven cases and who examines in three ways is called consummate, accomplished, a supreme person."

MAGGA SAMYUTTA: ON THE PATH

Avijjasutta:

Ignorance

So I have heard.

At one time the Buddha was staying near Savatthī in Jeta's Grove, Anathapindika's monastery.

There the Buddha addressed the mendicants,

"Mendicants!"

"Venerable sir," they replied.

The Buddha said this:

"Mendicants, ignorance precedes the attainment of unskillful qualities, with lack of conscience and prudence following along.

An ignoramus, sunk in ignorance, gives rise to wrong view.

Wrong view gives rise to wrong thought.

Wrong thought gives rise to wrong speech.

Wrong speech gives rise to wrong action.

Wrong action gives rise to wrong livelihood.

Wrong livelihood gives rise to wrong effort.

Wrong effort gives rise to wrong mindfulness.

Wrong mindfulness gives rise to wrong immersion.

Knowledge precedes the attainment of skillful qualities, with conscience and prudence following along.

A sage, firm in knowledge, gives rise to right view.

Right view gives rise to right thought.

Right thought gives rise to right speech.

Right speech gives rise to right action.

Right action gives rise to right livelihood.

Right livelihood gives rise to right effort.

Right effort gives rise to right mindfulness.

Right mindfulness gives rise to right immersion."

 Upaddhasutta:

Half the Spiritual Life

So I have heard.

At one time the Buddha was staying in the land of the Sakyans, where they have a town named Townsville.

Then Venerable Ananda went up to the Buddha, bowed, sat down to one side, and said to him:

"Sir, good friends, companions, and associates are half the spiritual life."

"Not so, Ananda! Not so, Ananda!

Good friends, companions, and associates are the whole of the spiritual life.

A mendicant with good friends, companions, and associates can expect to develop and cultivate the noble eightfold path.

And how does a mendicant with good friends develop and cultivate the noble eightfold path?

It's when a mendicant develops right view, which relies on seclusion, fading away, and cessation, and ripens as letting go.

They develop right thought …

right speech …

right action …

right livelihood …

right effort …

right mindfulness …

right immersion, which relies on seclusion, fading away, and cessation, and ripens as letting go.

That's how a mendicant with good friends develops and cultivates the noble eightfold path.

And here's another way to understand how good friends are the whole of the spiritual life.

For, by relying on me as a good friend, sentient beings who are liable to rebirth, old age, and death, to sorrow, lamentation, pain, sadness, and distress are freed from all these things.

This is another way to understand how good friends are the whole of the spiritual life."

 Sariputtasutta:

Sariputta

At Savatthī.

Then Sariputta went up to the Buddha, bowed, sat down to one side, and said to him:

"Sir, good friends, companions, and associates are the whole of the spiritual life."

"Good, good, Sariputta!

Good friends, companions, and associates are the whole of the spiritual life.

A mendicant with good friends, companions, and associates can expect to develop and cultivate the noble eightfold path.

And how does a mendicant with good friends develop and cultivate the noble eightfold path?

It's when a mendicant develops right view, right thought, right speech, right action, right livelihood, right effort, right mindfulness, and right immersion, which rely on seclusion, fading away, and cessation, and ripen as letting go.

That's how a mendicant with good friends develops and cultivates the noble eightfold path.

And here's another way to understand how good friends are the whole of the spiritual life.

For, by relying on me as a good friend, sentient beings who are liable to rebirth, old age, and death, to sorrow, lamentation, pain, sadness, and distress are freed from all these things.

This is another way to understand how good friends are the whole of the spiritual life."

Janussonibrahmanasutta:

Regarding the Brahmin Janussoni

At Savatthī.

Then Venerable Ananda robed up in the morning and, taking his bowl and robe, entered Savatthī for alms.

He saw the brahmin Janussoni driving out of Savatthī in a splendid all-white chariot drawn by mares.

The yoked horses were pure white, as were the ornaments, chariot, upholstery, reins, goad, and canopy. And his turban, robes, sandals were white, as was the chowry fanning him.

When people saw it they exclaimed,

"Wow! That's a Brahma vehicle!

It's a vehicle fit for Brahma!"

Then Ananda wandered for alms in Savatthī. After the meal, on his return from almsround, he went to the Buddha, bowed, sat down to one side, and told him what had happened, adding,

"Sir, can you point out a Brahma vehicle in this teaching and training?"

"I can, Ananda," said the Buddha.

"These are all terms for the noble eightfold path:

'vehicle of Brahma', or else 'vehicle of truth', or else 'supreme victory in battle'.

When right view is developed and cultivated it culminates with the removal of greed, hate, and delusion.

When right thought ...

right speech ...

right action ...

right livelihood ...

right effort …

right mindfulness …

right immersion is developed and cultivated it culminates with the removal of greed, hate, and delusion.

This is a way to understand how these are all terms for the noble eightfold path:

'vehicle of Brahma', or else 'vehicle of truth', or else 'supreme victory in battle'."

That is what the Buddha said.

Then the Holy One, the Teacher, went on to say:

"Its qualities of faith and wisdom

are always yoked to the shaft.

Conscience is its pole, mind its strap,

and mindfulness its careful driver.

The chariot's equipped with ethics,

its axle is absorption, and energy its wheel.

Equanimity and immersion are the carriage-shaft,

and it's upholstered with desirelessness.

Good will, harmlessness, and seclusion

are its weapons,

patience its shield and armor,

as it rolls on to sanctuary.

This supreme Brahma vehicle

arises in oneself.

The wise leave the world in it,

sure of winning the victory."

Kimatthiyasutta:

What's the Purpose

At Savatthī.

Then several mendicants went up to the Buddha … and said to him:

"Sir, sometimes wanderers of other religions ask us:

'Reverends, what's the purpose of leading the spiritual life under the ascetic Gotama?'

We answer them like this:

'The purpose of leading the spiritual life under the Buddha is to completely understand suffering.'

Answering this way, we trust that we repeat what the Buddha has said, and don't misrepresent him with an untruth. We trust our explanation is in line with the teaching, and that there are no legitimate grounds for rebuke or criticism."

"Indeed, in answering this way you repeat what I've said, and don't misrepresent me with an untruth. Your explanation is in line with the teaching, and there are no legitimate grounds for rebuke or criticism.

For the purpose of leading the spiritual life under me is to completely understand suffering.

If wanderers of other religions were to ask you:

'Is there a path and a practice for completely understanding that suffering?' You should answer them like this:

'There is.'

And what is that path?

It is simply this noble eightfold path, that is:

right view, right thought, right speech, right action, right livelihood, right effort, right mindfulness, and right immersion.

This is the path and the practice for completely understanding suffering.

When questioned by wanderers of other religions, that's how you should answer them."

Pathamaannatarabhikkhusutta:

A Mendicant (1st)

At Savatthī.

Then a mendicant went up to the Buddha … and asked him,

"Sir, they speak of this thing called the 'spiritual path'.

What is the spiritual path? And what is the culmination of the spiritual path?"

"Mendicant, the spiritual path is simply this noble eightfold path, that is:

right view, right thought, right speech, right action, right livelihood, right effort, right mindfulness, and right immersion.

The ending of greed, hate, and delusion.

This is the culmination of the spiritual path."

Dutiyaannatarabhikkhusutta:

A Mendicant (2nd)

At Savatthī.

Then a mendicant went up to the Buddha … and said to him:

"Sir, they speak of 'the removal of greed, hate, and delusion'.

What is this a term for?"

"Mendicant, the removal of greed, hate, and delusion is a term for the element of extinguishment.

It's used to speak of the ending of defilements."

When he said this, the mendicant said to the Buddha:

"Sir, they speak of 'the deathless'.

What is the deathless? And what is the path that leads to the deathless?"

"The ending of greed, hate, and delusion.

This is called the deathless.

The path that leads to the deathless is simply this noble eightfold path, that is:

right view, right thought, right speech, right action, right livelihood, right effort, right mindfulness, and right immersion."

Vibhangasutta:

Analysis

At Savatthī.

"Mendicants, I will teach and analyze for you the noble eightfold path.

Listen and pay close attention, I will speak."

"Yes, sir," they replied.

The Buddha said this:

"And what is the noble eightfold path?

It is right view, right thought, right speech, right action, right livelihood, right effort, right mindfulness, and right immersion.

And what is right view?

Knowing about suffering, the origin of suffering, the cessation of suffering, and the practice that leads to the cessation of suffering.

This is called right view.

And what is right thought?

It is the thought of renunciation, good will, and harmlessness.

This is called right thought.

And what is right speech?

Avoiding speech that's false, divisive, harsh, or nonsensical.

This is called right speech.

And what is right action?

Avoiding killing living creatures, stealing, and sexual activity.

This is called right action.

And what is right livelihood?

It's when a noble disciple gives up wrong livelihood and earns a living by right livelihood.

This is called right livelihood.

And what is right effort?

It's when a mendicant generates enthusiasm, tries, makes an effort, exerts the mind, and strives so that bad, unskillful qualities don't arise.

They generate enthusiasm, try, make an effort, exert the mind, and strive so that bad, unskillful qualities that have arisen are given up.

They generate enthusiasm, try, make an effort, exert the mind, and strive so that skillful qualities that have not arisen do arise.

They generate enthusiasm, try, make an effort, exert the mind, and strive so that skillful qualities that have arisen remain, are not lost, but increase, mature, and are fulfilled by development.

This is called right effort.

And what is right mindfulness?

It's when a mendicant meditates by observing an aspect of the body—keen, aware, and mindful, rid of desire and aversion for the world.

They meditate observing an aspect of feelings—keen, aware, and mindful, rid of desire and aversion for the world.

They meditate observing an aspect of the mind—keen, aware, and mindful, rid of desire and aversion for the world.

They meditate observing an aspect of principles—keen, aware, and mindful, rid of desire and aversion for the world.

This is called right mindfulness.

And what is right immersion?

It's when a mendicant, quite secluded from sensual pleasures, secluded from unskillful qualities, enters and remains in the first absorption, which has the rapture and bliss born of seclusion, while placing the mind and keeping it connected.

As the placing of the mind and keeping it connected are stilled, they enter and remain in the second absorption, which has the rapture and bliss born of immersion, with internal clarity and confidence, and unified mind, without placing the mind and keeping it connected.

And with the fading away of rapture, they enter and remain in the third absorption, where they meditate with equanimity, mindful and aware, personally experiencing the bliss of which the noble ones declare, 'Equanimous and mindful, one meditates in bliss.'

Giving up pleasure and pain, and ending former happiness and sadness, they enter and remain in the fourth absorption, without pleasure or pain, with pure equanimity and mindfulness.

This is called right immersion."

Sukasutta:

A Spike

At Savatthī.

"Mendicants, suppose a spike of rice or barley was pointing the wrong way. If you trod on it with hand or foot, there's no way it could break the skin and produce blood.

Why is that?

Because the spike is pointing the wrong way.

In the same way, a mendicant whose view and development of the path is pointing the wrong way cannot break ignorance, produce knowledge, and realize extinguishment.

Why is that?

Because their view is pointing the wrong way.

Suppose a spike of rice or barley was pointing the right way. If you trod on it with hand or foot, it may well break the skin and produce blood.

Why is that?

Because the spike is pointing the right way.

In the same way, a mendicant whose view and development of the path is pointing the right way may well break ignorance, produce knowledge, and realize extinguishment.

Why is that?

Because their view is pointing the right way.

And how does a mendicant whose view and development of the path is pointing the right way break ignorance, give rise to knowledge, and realize extinguishment?

It's when a mendicant develops right view, right thought, right speech, right action, right livelihood, right effort, right mindfulness, and right immersion, which rely on seclusion, fading away, and cessation, and ripen as letting go.

That's how a mendicant whose view and development of the path is pointing the right way breaks ignorance, gives rise to knowledge, and realizes extinguishment."

Nandiyasutta:

With Nandiya

At Savatthī.

Then the wanderer Nandiya went up to the Buddha, and exchanged greetings with him.

When the greetings and polite conversation were over, he sat down to one side, and said to the Buddha:

"Master Gotama, how many things, when developed and cultivated, have extinguishment as their culmination, destination, and end?"

"These eight things, when developed and cultivated, have extinguishment as their culmination, destination, and end.

What eight?

They are: right view, right thought, right speech, right action, right livelihood, right effort, right mindfulness, and right immersion.

These eight things, when developed and cultivated, have extinguishment as their culmination, destination, and end."

When he said this, the wanderer Nandiya said to the Buddha,

"Excellent, Master Gotama! Excellent! …

From this day forth, may Master Gotama remember me as a lay follower who has gone for refuge for life."

Pathamaviharasutta:

Meditation (1st)

At Savatthī.

"Mendicants, I wish to go on retreat for a fortnight.

No-one should approach me, except for the one who brings my almsfood."

"Yes, sir," replied those mendicants. And no-one approached him, except for the one who brought the almsfood.

Then after a fortnight had passed, the Buddha came out of retreat and addressed the mendicants:

"Mendicants, I've been practicing part of the meditation I practiced when I was first awakened.

I understand that

there's feeling conditioned by wrong view

and feeling conditioned by right view. …

There's feeling conditioned by wrong immersion,

and feeling conditioned by right immersion.

There's feeling conditioned by desire,

by thought,

and by perception.

As long as desire, thought, and perception are not stilled, there is feeling conditioned by that.

When desire, thought, and perception are stilled, there is feeling conditioned by that.

There is effort to attain the unattained. When that state has been attained, there is also feeling conditioned by that."

Dutiyaviharasutta:

Meditation (2nd)

At Savatthī.

"Mendicants, I wish to go on retreat for three months.

No-one should approach me, except for the one who brings my almsfood."

"Yes, sir," replied those mendicants. And no-one approached him, except for the one who brought the almsfood.

Then after three months had passed, the Buddha came out of retreat and addressed the mendicants:

"Mendicants, I've been practicing part of the meditation I practiced when I was first awakened.

I understand that

there's feeling conditioned by wrong view

and by the stilling of wrong view,

by right view

and by the stilling of right view. …

There's feeling conditioned by wrong immersion

and by the stilling of wrong immersion, by right immersion

and by the stilling of right immersion.

There's feeling conditioned by desire

and by the stilling of desire,

by thought

and by the stilling of thought,

by perception

and by the stilling of perception.

As long as desire, thought, and perception are not stilled, there is feeling conditioned by that.

When desire, thought, and perception are stilled, there is feeling conditioned by that.

There is effort to attain the unattained. When that state has been attained, there is also feeling conditioned by that."

Sekkhasutta:

A Trainee

At Savatthī.

Then a mendicant went up to the Buddha … and asked him,

"Sir, they speak of this person called 'a trainee'.

How is a trainee defined?"

"Mendicant, it's someone who has a trainee's right view, right thought, right speech, right action, right livelihood, right effort, right mindfulness, and right immersion.

That's how a trainee is defined."

Pathamauppadasutta:

Arising (1st)

At Savatthī.

"Mendicants, these eight things don't arise to be developed and cultivated except when a Realized One, a perfected one, a fully awakened Buddha has appeared.

What eight?

They are: right view, right thought, right speech, right action, right livelihood, right effort, right mindfulness, and right immersion.

These eight things don't arise to be developed and cultivated except when a Realized One, a perfected one, a fully awakened Buddha has appeared."

Dutiyauppadasutta:

Arising (2nd)

At Savatthī.

"Mendicants, these eight things don't arise to be developed and cultivated apart from the Holy One's training.

What eight?

They are: right view, right thought, right speech, right action, right livelihood, right effort, right mindfulness, and right immersion.

These are the eight things that don't arise to be developed and cultivated apart from the Holy One's training."

Pathamaparisuddhasutta:

Purified (1st)

At Savatthī.

"Mendicants, these eight things don't arise to be purified, bright, flawless, and rid of corruptions except when a Realized One, a perfected one, a fully awakened Buddha has appeared.

What eight?

They are: right view, right thought, right speech, right action, right livelihood, right effort, right mindfulness, and right immersion.

These eight things don't arise to be purified, bright, flawless, and rid of corruptions except when a Realized One, a perfected one, a fully awakened Buddha has appeared."

Dutiyaparisuddhasutta:

Purified (2nd)

At Savatthī.

"Mendicants, these eight things don't arise to be purified, bright, flawless, and rid of corruptions apart from the Holy One's training.

What eight?

They are: right view, right thought, right speech, right action, right livelihood, right effort, right mindfulness, and right immersion.

These eight things don't arise to be purified, bright, flawless, and rid of corruptions apart from the Holy One's training."

Pathamakukkutaramasutta:

At the Chicken Monastery (1st)

So I have heard.

At one time the venerables Ananda and Bhadda were staying near Pataliputta, in the Chicken Monastery.

Then in the late afternoon, Venerable Bhadda came out of retreat, went to Venerable Ananda, and exchanged greetings with him.

When the greetings and polite conversation were over, he sat down to one side and said to Ananda:

"Reverend, they speak of this thing called 'not the spiritual path'.

What is not the spiritual path?"

"Good, good, Reverend Bhadda!

Your approach and articulation are excellent, and it's a good question.

For you asked:

'They speak of this thing called "not the spiritual path".

What is not the spiritual path?'"

"Yes, reverend."

"What is not the spiritual path is simply the wrong eightfold path, that is:

wrong view, wrong thought, wrong speech, wrong action, wrong livelihood, wrong effort, wrong mindfulness, and wrong immersion."

 Dutiyakukkutaramasutta:

At the Chicken Monastery (2nd)

At Pataliputta.

"Reverend, they speak of this thing called the 'spiritual path'.

What is the spiritual path? And what is the culmination of the spiritual path?"

"Good, good, Reverend Bhadda!

Your approach and articulation are excellent, and it's a good question.

For you asked:

'They speak of this thing called "the spiritual path".

What is the spiritual path? And what is the culmination of the spiritual path?'"

"Yes, reverend."

"The spiritual path is simply this noble eightfold path, that is:

right view, right thought, right speech, right action, right livelihood, right effort, right mindfulness, and right immersion.

The ending of greed, hate, and delusion:

this is the culmination of the spiritual path."

Tatiyakukkutaramasutta:

At the Chicken Monastery (3rd)

At Pataliputta.

"Reverend, they speak of this thing called the 'spiritual path'.

What is the spiritual path? Who is someone on the spiritual path? And what is the culmination of the spiritual path?"

"Good, good, Reverend Bhadda!

Your approach and articulation are excellent, and it's a good question. …

The spiritual path is simply this noble eightfold path, that is:

right view, right thought, right speech, right action, right livelihood, right effort, right mindfulness, and right immersion.

Someone who possesses this noble eightfold path

is called someone on the spiritual path.

The ending of greed, hate, and delusion:

this is the culmination of the spiritual path."

Micchattasutta:

The Wrong Way

At Savatthī.

"Mendicants, I will teach you the wrong way and the right way.

Listen …

And what is the wrong way?

It is wrong view, wrong thought, wrong speech, wrong action, wrong livelihood, wrong effort, wrong mindfulness, and wrong immersion.

This is called the wrong way.

And what is the right way?

It is right view, right thought, right speech, right action, right livelihood, right effort, right mindfulness, and right immersion.

This is called the right way."

Akusaladhammasutta:

Unskillful Qualities

At Savatthī.

"Mendicants, I will teach you skillful and unskillful qualities.

Listen …

And what are unskillful qualities?

They are wrong view, wrong thought, wrong speech, wrong action, wrong livelihood, wrong effort, wrong mindfulness, and wrong immersion.

These are called unskillful qualities.

And what are skillful qualities?

They are right view, right thought, right speech, right action, right livelihood, right effort, right mindfulness, and right immersion.

These are called skillful qualities."

Pathamapatipadasutta:

Practice (1st)

At Savatthī.

"Mendicants, I will teach you the wrong practice and the right practice.

Listen …

And what's the wrong practice?

It is wrong view, wrong thought, wrong speech, wrong action, wrong livelihood, wrong effort, wrong mindfulness, and wrong immersion.

This is called the wrong practice.

And what's the right practice?

It is right view, right thought, right speech, right action, right livelihood, right effort, right mindfulness, and right immersion.

This is called the right practice."

Dutiyapatipadasutta:

Practice (2nd)

At Savatthī.

"Mendicants, I don't praise wrong practice for laypeople or renunciates.

Because of wrong practice, neither laypeople nor renunciates succeed in the procedure of the skillful teaching.

And what's the wrong practice?

It is wrong view, wrong thought, wrong speech, wrong action, wrong livelihood, wrong effort, wrong mindfulness, and wrong immersion.

This is called the wrong practice.

I don't praise wrong practice for lay people or renunciates.

Because of wrong practice, neither laypeople nor renunciates succeed in the procedure of the skillful teaching.

I praise right practice for laypeople and renunciates.

Because of right practice, both laypeople and renunciates succeed in the procedure of the skillful teaching.

And what's the right practice?

It is right view, right thought, right speech, right action, right livelihood, right effort, right mindfulness, and right immersion.

This is called the right practice.

I praise right practice for laypeople and renunciates.

Because of right practice, both laypeople and renunciates succeed in the procedure of the skillful teaching."

Pathamaasappurisasutta:

A Good Person (1st)

At Savatthī.

"Mendicants, I will teach you a bad person and a good person.

Listen …

And what is a bad person?

It's someone who has wrong view, wrong thought, wrong speech, wrong action, wrong livelihood, wrong effort, wrong mindfulness, and wrong immersion.

This is called a bad person.

And what is a good person?

It's someone who has right view, right thought, right speech, right action, right livelihood, right effort, right mindfulness, and right immersion.

This is called a good person."

Dutiyaasappurisasutta:

A Good Person (2nd)

At Savatthī.

"Mendicants, I will teach you a bad person and a worse person,

a good person and a better person.

Listen …

And what is a bad person?

It's someone who has wrong view, wrong thought, wrong speech, wrong action, wrong livelihood, wrong effort, wrong mindfulness, and wrong immersion.

This is called a bad person.

And what is a worse person?

It's someone who has wrong view, wrong thought, wrong speech, wrong action, wrong livelihood, wrong effort, wrong mindfulness, wrong immersion, wrong knowledge, and wrong freedom.

This is called a worse person.

And what is a good person?

It's someone who has right view, right thought, right speech, right action, right livelihood, right effort, right mindfulness, and right immersion.

This is called a good person.

And what is a better person?

It's someone who has right view, right thought, right speech, right action, right livelihood, right effort, right mindfulness, right immersion, right knowledge, and right freedom.

This is called a better person."

Kumbhasutta:

Pots

At Savatthī.

"A pot without a stand is easy to overturn, but if it has a stand it's hard to overturn.

In the same way, a mind without a stand is easy to overturn, but if it has a stand it's hard to overturn.

And what's the stand for the mind?

It is simply this noble eightfold path, that is:

right view, right thought, right speech, right action, right livelihood, right effort, right mindfulness, and right immersion.

This is the stand for the mind.

A pot without a stand is easy to overturn, but if it has a stand it's hard to overturn.

In the same way, a mind without a stand is easy to overturn, but if it has a stand it's hard to overturn."

Samadhisutta:

Immersion

At Savatthī.

"Mendicants, I will teach you noble right immersion with its vital conditions and its prerequisites.

Listen …

And what is noble right immersion with its vital conditions and its prerequisites?

There are right view, right thought, right speech, right action, right livelihood, right effort, and right mindfulness.

Unification of mind with these seven factors as prerequisites is called noble right immersion 'with its vital conditions' and 'with its prerequisites'."

Vedanasutta:

Feeling

At Savatthī.

"Mendicants, there are these three feelings.

What three?

Pleasant, painful, and neutral feeling.

These are the three feelings.

The noble eightfold path should be developed to completely understand these three feelings.

What is the noble eightfold path?

It is right view, right thought, right speech, right action, right livelihood, right effort, right mindfulness, and right immersion.

This noble eightfold path should be developed to completely understand these three feelings."

Uttiyasutta:

With Uttiya

At Savatthī.

Then Venerable Uttiya went up to the Buddha … and asked him,

"Just now, sir, as I was in private retreat this thought came to mind.

'The Buddha has spoken of the five kinds of sensual stimulation.

What are they?'"

"Good, good, Uttiya!

I have spoken of these five kinds of sensual stimulation.

What five?

Sights known by the eye that are likable, desirable, agreeable, pleasant, sensual, and arousing.

Sounds known by the ear …

Smells known by the nose …

Tastes known by the tongue …

Touches known by the body that are likable, desirable, agreeable, pleasant, sensual, and arousing.

These are the five kinds of sensual stimulation that I've spoken of.

The noble eightfold path should be developed to give up these five kinds of sensual stimulation.

What is the noble eightfold path?

It is right view, right thought, right speech, right action, right livelihood, right effort, right mindfulness, and right immersion.

This is the noble eightfold path that should be developed to give up these five kinds of sensual stimulation."

Pathamapatipattisutta:

Practice (1st)

At Savatthī.

"Mendicants, I will teach you the wrong practice and the right practice.

Listen …

And what's the wrong practice?

It is wrong view, wrong thought, wrong speech, wrong action, wrong livelihood, wrong effort, wrong mindfulness, and wrong immersion.

This is called the wrong practice.

And what's the right practice?

It is right view, right thought, right speech, right action, right livelihood, right effort, right mindfulness, and right immersion.

This is called the right practice."

Dutiyapatipattisutta:

Practice (2nd)

At Savatthī.

"Mendicants, I will teach you one practicing wrongly and one practicing rightly.

Listen …

And who is practicing wrongly?

It's someone who has wrong view, wrong thought, wrong speech, wrong action, wrong livelihood, wrong effort, wrong mindfulness, and wrong immersion.

This is called one practicing wrongly.

And who is practicing rightly?

It's someone who has right view, right thought, right speech, right action, right livelihood, right effort, right mindfulness, and right immersion.

This is called one practicing rightly."

Viraddhasutta:

Missed Out

At Savatthī.

"Mendicants, whoever has missed out on the noble eightfold path has missed out on the noble path to the complete ending of suffering.

Whoever has undertaken the noble eightfold path has undertaken the noble path to the complete ending of suffering.

And what is the noble eightfold path?

It is right view, right thought, right speech, right action, right livelihood, right effort, right mindfulness, and right immersion.

Whoever has missed out on the noble eightfold path has missed out on the noble path to the complete ending of suffering.

Whoever has undertaken the noble eightfold path has undertaken the noble path to the complete ending of suffering."

Parangamasutta:

Going to the Far Shore

At Savatthī.

"Mendicants, when these eight things are developed and cultivated they lead to going from the near shore to the far shore.

What eight?

They are right view, right thought, right speech, right action, right livelihood, right effort, right mindfulness, and right immersion.

When these eight things are developed and cultivated they lead to going from the near shore to the far shore."

That is what the Buddha said.

Then the Holy One, the Teacher, went on to say:

"Few are those among humans

who cross to the far shore.

The rest just run

around on the near shore.

When the teaching is well explained,

those who practice accordingly

are the ones who will cross over

Death's domain so hard to pass.

Rid of dark qualities,

an astute person should develop the bright.

Leaving home behind

for the seclusion so hard to enjoy,

you should try to find delight there,

having left behind sensual pleasures.

With no possessions, an astute person

should cleanse themselves of mental corruptions.

And those whose minds are rightly developed

in the awakening factors;

letting go of attachments,

they delight in not grasping.

With defilements ended, brilliant,

they are extinguished in this world."

Pathamasamannasutta:

The Ascetic Life (1st)

At Savatthī.

"Mendicants, I will teach you the ascetic life and the fruits of the ascetic life.

Listen …

And what is the ascetic life?

It is simply this noble eightfold path, that is:

right view, right thought, right speech, right action, right livelihood, right effort, right mindfulness, and right immersion.

This is called the ascetic life.

And what are the fruits of the ascetic life?

The fruits of stream-entry, once-return, non-return, and perfection.

These are called the fruits of the ascetic life."

Dutiyasamannasutta:

The Ascetic Life (2nd)

At Savatthī.

"Mendicants, I will teach you the ascetic life and the goal of the ascetic life.

Listen …

And what is the ascetic life?

It is simply this noble eightfold path, that is:

right view, right thought, right speech, right action, right livelihood, right effort, right mindfulness, and right immersion.

This is called the ascetic life.

And what is the goal of the ascetic life?

The ending of greed, hate, and delusion.

This is called the goal of the ascetic life."

Pathamabrahmannasutta:

The Brahmin Life (1st)

At Savatthī.

"Mendicants, I will teach you life as a brahmin and the fruits of life as a brahmin.

Listen …

And what is life as a brahmin?

It is simply this noble eightfold path, that is:

right view, right thought, right speech, right action, right livelihood, right effort, right mindfulness, and right immersion.

This is called life as a brahmin.

And what are the fruits of life as a brahmin?

The fruits of stream-entry, once-return, non-return, and perfection.

These are called the fruits of life as a brahmin."

Dutiyabrahmannasutta:

The Brahmin Life (2nd)

At Savatthī.

"Mendicants, I will teach you life as a brahmin and the goal of life as a brahmin.

Listen …

And what is life as a brahmin?

It is simply this noble eightfold path, that is:

right view, right thought, right speech, right action, right livelihood, right effort, right mindfulness, and right immersion.

This is called life as a brahmin.

And what is the goal of life as a brahmin?

The ending of greed, hate, and delusion.

This is called the goal of life as a brahmin."

Pathamabrahmacariyasutta:

The Spiritual Path (1st)

At Savatthī.

"Mendicants, I will teach you the spiritual path and the fruits of the spiritual path.

Listen …

And what is the spiritual path?

It is simply this noble eightfold path, that is:

right view, right thought, right speech, right action, right livelihood, right effort, right mindfulness, and right immersion.

This is called the spiritual path.

And what are the fruits of the spiritual path?

The fruits of stream-entry, once-return, non-return, and perfection.

These are called the fruits of the spiritual path."

Dutiyabrahmacariyasutta:

The Spiritual Path (2nd)

At Savatthī.

"Mendicants, I will teach you the spiritual path and the goal of the spiritual path.

Listen …

And what is the spiritual path?

It is simply this noble eightfold path, that is:

right view, right thought, right speech, right action, right livelihood, right effort, right mindfulness, and right immersion.

This is called the spiritual path.

And what is the goal of the spiritual path?

The ending of greed, hate, and delusion.

This is called the goal of the spiritual path."

Ragaviragasutta:

The Fading Away of Greed

At Savatthī.

"Mendicants, if wanderers who follow another religion were to ask you:

'Reverends, what's the purpose of leading the spiritual life under the ascetic Gotama?' You should answer them like this:

'The purpose of leading the spiritual life under the Buddha is the fading away of greed.'

If wanderers of other religions were to ask you:

'Is there a path and a practice for the fading away of greed?' You should answer them like this:

'There is a path and a practice for the fading away of greed.'

And what is that path, what is that practice for the fading away of greed?

It is simply this noble eightfold path, that is:

right view, right thought, right speech, right action, right livelihood, right effort, right mindfulness, and right immersion.

This is the path, this is the practice for the fading away of greed.

When questioned by wanderers of other religions, that's how you should answer them."

Samyojanappahanadisuttachakka:

Six Discourses on Giving Up Fetters, Etc.

"Mendicants, if wanderers who follow another religion were to ask you:

'Reverends, what's the purpose of leading the spiritual life under the ascetic Gotama?' You should answer them like this:

'The purpose of leading the spiritual life under the Buddha is to give up the fetters.' …

'… to uproot the underlying tendencies.' …

'… to completely understand the course of time.' …

'… to end the defilements.' …

'… to realize the fruit of knowledge and freedom.' …

'… for knowledge and vision.' …"

Anupadaparinibbanasutta:

Extinguishment by Not Grasping

At Savatthī.

"Mendicants, if wanderers who follow another religion were to ask you:

'Reverends, what's the purpose of leading the spiritual life under the ascetic Gotama?' You should answer them like this:

'The purpose of leading the spiritual life under the Buddha is extinguishment by not grasping.'

If wanderers of other religions were to ask you:

'Is there a path and a practice for extinguishment by not grasping?' You should answer them like this:

'There is a path and a practice for extinguishment by not grasping.'

And what is that path, what is that practice for extinguishment by not grasping?

It is simply this noble eightfold path, that is:

right view, right thought, right speech, right action, right livelihood, right effort, right mindfulness, and right immersion.

This is the path, this is the practice for extinguishment by not grasping.

When questioned by wanderers of other religions, that's how you should answer them."

Kalyanamittasutta:

Good Friends (1st)

At Savatthī.

"Mendicants, the dawn is the forerunner and precursor of the sunrise.

In the same way good friendship is the forerunner and precursor of the noble eightfold path for a mendicant.

A mendicant with good friends can expect to develop and cultivate the noble eightfold path.

And how does a mendicant with good friends develop and cultivate the noble eightfold path?

It's when a mendicant develops right view, right thought, right speech, right action, right livelihood, right effort, right mindfulness, and right immersion, which rely on seclusion, fading away, and cessation, and ripen as letting go.

That's how a mendicant with good friends develops and cultivates the noble eightfold path."

Sīlasampadadisuttapancaka:

Five Discourses on Accomplishment in Ethics, Etc. (1st)

"Mendicants, the dawn is the forerunner and precursor of the sunrise.

In the same way accomplishment in ethics is the forerunner and precursor of the noble eightfold path for a mendicant.

A mendicant accomplished in ethics can expect …" …

"… accomplished in enthusiasm …"

"… accomplished in self-development …"

"… accomplished in view …"

"… accomplished in diligence …"

Yonisomanasikarasampadasutta:

Accomplishment in Proper Attention (1st)

"Mendicants, the dawn is the forerunner and precursor of the sunrise.

In the same way accomplishment in proper attention is the forerunner and precursor of the noble eightfold path for a mendicant.

A mendicant accomplished in proper attention can expect to develop and cultivate the noble eightfold path.

And how does a mendicant accomplished in proper attention develop and cultivate the noble eightfold path?

It's when a mendicant develops right view, right thought, right speech, right action, right livelihood, right effort, right mindfulness, and right immersion, which rely on seclusion, fading away, and cessation, and ripen as letting go.

That's how a mendicant accomplished in proper attention develops and cultivates the noble eightfold path."

Dutiyakalyanamittasutta:

Good Friends (2nd)

"Mendicants, the dawn is the forerunner and precursor of the sunrise.

In the same way good friendship is the forerunner and precursor of the noble eightfold path for a mendicant.

A mendicant with good friends can expect to develop and cultivate the noble eightfold path.

And how does a mendicant with good friends develop and cultivate the noble eightfold path?

It's when a mendicant develops right view, right thought, right speech, right action, right livelihood, right effort, right mindfulness, and right immersion, which culminate in the removal of greed, hate, and delusion.

That's how a mendicant with good friends develops and cultivates the noble eightfold path."

Dutiyasīlasampadadisuttapancaka:

Five Discourses on Accomplishment in Ethics, Etc. (2nd)

"Mendicants, the dawn is the forerunner and precursor of the sunrise.

In the same way accomplishment in ethics is the forerunner and precursor of the noble eightfold path for a mendicant. …"

"… accomplishment in enthusiasm …"

"… accomplishment in self-development …"

"… accomplishment in view …"

"… accomplishment in diligence …"

 Dutiyayonisomanasikarasampadasutta:

Accomplishment in Proper Attention (2nd)

"… accomplishment in proper attention.

A mendicant accomplished in proper attention can expect to develop and cultivate the noble eightfold path.

And how does a mendicant accomplished in proper attention develop and cultivate the noble eightfold path?

It's when a mendicant develops right view, right thought, right speech, right action, right livelihood, right effort, right mindfulness, and right immersion, which culminate in the removal of greed, hate, and delusion.

That's how a mendicant accomplished in proper attention develops and cultivates the noble eightfold path."

Kalyanamittasutta:

Good Friends (1st)

At Savatthī.

"Mendicants, one thing helps give rise to the noble eightfold path.

What one thing?

It's good friendship.

A mendicant with good friends can expect to develop and cultivate the noble eightfold path.

And how does a mendicant with good friends develop and cultivate the noble eightfold path?

It's when a mendicant develops right view, right thought, right speech, right action, right livelihood, right effort, right mindfulness, and right immersion, which rely on seclusion, fading away, and cessation, and ripen as letting go.

That's how a mendicant with good friends develops and cultivates the noble eightfold path."

Sīlasampadadisuttapancaka:

Five Discourses on Accomplishment in Ethics, Etc. (1st)

"Mendicants, one thing helps give rise to the noble eightfold path.

What one thing?

It's accomplishment in ethics. …"

"… accomplishment in enthusiasm …"

"… accomplishment in self-development …"

"… accomplishment in view …"

"… accomplishment in diligence …"

Yonisomanasikarasampadasutta:

Accomplishment in Proper Attention (1st)

"… accomplishment in proper attention.

A mendicant accomplished in proper attention can expect to develop and cultivate the noble eightfold path.

And how does a mendicant accomplished in proper attention develop and cultivate the noble eightfold path?

It's when a mendicant develops right view, right thought, right speech, right action, right livelihood, right effort, right mindfulness, and right immersion, which rely on seclusion, fading away, and cessation, and ripen as letting go.

That's how a mendicant accomplished in proper attention develops and cultivates the noble eightfold path."

Dutiyakalyanamittasutta:

Good Friends (2nd)

At Savatthī.

"Mendicants, one thing helps give rise to the noble eightfold path.

What one thing?

It's good friendship.

A mendicant with good friends can expect to develop and cultivate the noble eightfold path.

And how does a mendicant with good friends develop and cultivate the noble eightfold path?

It's when a mendicant develops right view, right thought, right speech, right action, right livelihood, right effort, right mindfulness, and right immersion, which culminate in the removal of greed, hate, and delusion.

That's how a mendicant with good friends develops and cultivates the noble eightfold path."

Dutiyasīlasampadadisuttapancaka:

Five Discourses on Accomplishment in Ethics, Etc. (2nd)

At Savatthī.

"Mendicants, one thing helps give rise to the noble eightfold path.

What one thing?

It's accomplishment in ethics. …"

"… accomplishment in enthusiasm …"

"… accomplishment in self-development …"

"… accomplishment in view …"

"… accomplishment in diligence …"

Dutiyayonisomanasikarasampadasutta:

Accomplishment in Proper Attention (2nd)

"… accomplishment in proper attention.

A mendicant accomplished in proper attention can expect to develop and cultivate the noble eightfold path.

And how does a mendicant accomplished in proper attention develop and cultivate the noble eightfold path?

It's when a mendicant develops right view, right thought, right speech, right action, right livelihood, right effort, right mindfulness, and right immersion, which culminate in the removal of greed, hate, and delusion.

That's how a mendicant accomplished in proper attention develops and cultivates the noble eightfold path."

Kalyanamittasutta:

Good Friends

At Savatthī.

"Mendicants, I do not see a single thing that gives rise to the noble eightfold path, or, if it's already arisen, fully develops it like good friendship.

A mendicant with good friends can expect to develop and cultivate the noble eightfold path.

And how does a mendicant with good friends develop and cultivate the noble eightfold path?

It's when a mendicant develops right view, right thought, right speech, right action, right livelihood, right effort, right mindfulness, and right immersion, which rely on seclusion, fading away, and cessation, and ripen as letting go.

That's how a mendicant with good friends develops and cultivates the noble eightfold path."

Sīlasampadadisuttapancaka:

Five Discourses on Accomplishment in Ethics, Etc.

"Mendicants, I do not see a single thing that gives rise to the noble eightfold path, or, if it's already arisen, fully develops it like accomplishment in ethics. ..."

"... accomplishment in enthusiasm ..."

"... accomplishment in self-development ..."

"... accomplishment in view ..."

"... accomplishment in diligence ..."

Yonisomanasikarasampadasutta:

Accomplishment in Proper Attention

"… accomplishment in proper attention.

A mendicant accomplished in proper attention can expect to develop and cultivate the noble eightfold path.

And how does a mendicant accomplished in proper attention develop and cultivate the noble eightfold path?

It's when a mendicant develops right view, right thought, right speech, right action, right livelihood, right effort, right mindfulness, and right immersion, which rely on seclusion, fading away, and cessation, and ripen as letting go.

That's how a mendicant accomplished in proper attention develops and cultivates the noble eightfold path."

Dutiyakalyanamittasutta:

Good Friends (2nd)

"Mendicants, I do not see a single thing that gives rise to the noble eightfold path, or, if it's already arisen, fully develops it like good friendship.

A mendicant with good friends can expect to develop and cultivate the noble eightfold path.

And how does a mendicant with good friends develop and cultivate the noble eightfold path?

It's when a mendicant develops right view, right thought, right speech, right action, right livelihood, right effort, right mindfulness, and right immersion, which culminate in the removal of greed, hate, and delusion.

That's how a mendicant with good friends develops and cultivates the noble eightfold path."

Dutiyasīlasampadadisuttapancaka:

Five Discourses on Accomplishment in Ethics, Etc.

"Mendicants, I do not see a single thing that gives rise to the noble eightfold path, or, if it's already arisen, fully develops it like accomplishment in ethics. …"

"… accomplishment in enthusiasm …"

"… accomplishment in self-development …"

"… accomplishment in view …"

"… accomplishment in diligence …"

Dutiyayonisomanasikarasampadasutta:

Accomplishment in Proper Attention (2nd)

"… accomplishment in proper attention.

A mendicant accomplished in proper attention can expect to develop and cultivate the noble eightfold path.

And how does a mendicant accomplished in proper attention develop and cultivate the noble eightfold path?

It's when a mendicant develops right view, right thought, right speech, right action, right livelihood, right effort, right mindfulness, and right immersion, which culminate in the removal of greed, hate, and delusion.

That's how a mendicant accomplished in proper attention develops and cultivates the noble eightfold path."

Pathamapacīnaninnasutta:

Slanting East

At Savatthī.

"Mendicants, the Ganges river slants, slopes, and inclines to the east.

In the same way, a mendicant who develops and cultivates the noble eightfold path slants, slopes, and inclines to extinguishment.

And how does a mendicant who develops the noble eightfold path slant, slope, and incline to extinguishment?

It's when a mendicant develops right view, right thought, right speech, right action, right livelihood, right effort, right mindfulness, and right immersion, which rely on seclusion, fading away, and cessation, and ripen as letting go.

That's how a mendicant who develops and cultivates the noble eightfold path slants, slopes, and inclines to extinguishment."

Dutiyadipacīnaninnasuttacatukka:

Four Discourses on Slanting East

"Mendicants, the Yamuna river slants, slopes, and inclines to the east. …"

"… the Aciravatī river …"

"… the Sarabhu river …"

"… the Mahī river …"

Chatthapacīnaninnasutta:

Sixth Discourse on Slanting East

"Mendicants, all the great rivers—that is,

the Ganges, Yamuna, Aciravatī, Sarabhu, and Mahī—slant, slope, and incline towards the east.

In the same way, a mendicant who develops and cultivates the noble eightfold path slants, slopes, and inclines to extinguishment.

And how does a mendicant who develops the noble eightfold path slant, slope, and incline to extinguishment?

It's when a mendicant develops right view, right thought, right speech, right action, right livelihood, right effort, right mindfulness, and right immersion, which rely on seclusion, fading away, and cessation, and ripen as letting go.

That's how a mendicant who develops and cultivates the noble eightfold path slants, slopes, and inclines to extinguishment."

Pathamasamuddaninnasutta:

Slanting to the Ocean

"Mendicants, the Ganges river slants, slopes, and inclines to the ocean.

In the same way, a mendicant who develops the noble eightfold path slants, slopes, and inclines to extinguishment. ..."

Dutiyadisamuddaninnasuttapancaka:

Five Discourses on Slanting to the Ocean

"Mendicants, the Yamuna river slants, slopes, and inclines to the ocean. ..."

"... the Aciravatī river ..."

"... the Sarabhu river ..."

"... the Mahī river ..."

"... all the great rivers ..."

Pathamapacīnaninnasutta:

Slanting East

"Mendicants, the Ganges river slants, slopes, and inclines to the east.

In the same way, a mendicant who develops and cultivates the noble eightfold path slants, slopes, and inclines to extinguishment.

And how does a mendicant who develops the noble eightfold path slant, slope, and incline to extinguishment?

It's when a mendicant develops right view, right thought, right speech, right action, right livelihood, right effort, right mindfulness, and right immersion, which culminate in the removal of greed, hate, and delusion.

That's how a mendicant who develops and cultivates the noble eightfold path slants, slopes, and inclines to extinguishment."

Dutiyadipacīnaninnasuttapancaka:

Five Discourses on Sloping to the East

"Mendicants, the Yamuna river slants, slopes, and inclines to the east. …"

"… the Aciravatī river …"

"… the Sarabhu river …"

"… the Mahī river …"

"… all the great rivers …"

Pathamasamuddaninnasutta:

Slanting to the Ocean

"Mendicants, the Ganges river slants, slopes, and inclines to the ocean.

In the same way, a mendicant who develops and cultivates the noble eightfold path slants, slopes, and inclines to extinguishment.

And how does a mendicant who develops the noble eightfold path slant, slope, and incline to extinguishment?

It's when a mendicant develops right view, right thought, right speech, right action, right livelihood, right effort, right mindfulness, and right immersion, which culminate in the removal of greed, hate, and delusion.

That's how a mendicant who develops and cultivates the noble eightfold path slants, slopes, and inclines to extinguishment."

Dutiyadisamuddaninnasutta:

Slanting to the Ocean

"Mendicants, the Yamuna river slants, slopes, and inclines to the ocean. …"

"… the Aciravatī river …"

"… the Sarabhu river …"

"… the Mahī river …"

"… all the great rivers …"

Pathamapacīnaninnasutta:

Slanting East

"Mendicants, the Ganges river slants, slopes, and inclines to the east.

In the same way, a mendicant who develops and cultivates the noble eightfold path slants, slopes, and inclines to extinguishment.

And how does a mendicant who develops the noble eightfold path slant, slope, and incline to extinguishment?

It's when a mendicant develops right view, right thought, right speech, right action, right livelihood, right effort, right mindfulness, and right immersion, which culminate, finish, and end in the deathless.

That's how a mendicant who develops and cultivates the noble eightfold path slants, slopes, and inclines to extinguishment."

Dutiyadipacīnaninnasutta:

Slanting East

"Mendicants, the Yamuna river slants, slopes, and inclines to the east. ..."

"... the Aciravatī river ..."

"... the Sarabhu river ..."

"... the Mahī river ..."

"... all the great rivers ..."

Pathamasamuddaninnasutta:

Slanting to the Ocean

"Mendicants, the Ganges river slants, slopes, and inclines to the ocean.

In the same way, a mendicant who develops and cultivates the noble eightfold path slants, slopes, and inclines to extinguishment.

And how does a mendicant who develops the noble eightfold path slant, slope, and incline to extinguishment?

It's when a mendicant develops right view, right thought, right speech, right action, right livelihood, right effort, right mindfulness, and right immersion, which culminate, finish, and end in the deathless.

That's how a mendicant who develops and cultivates the noble eightfold path slants, slopes, and inclines to extinguishment."

Dutiyadisamuddaninnasutta:

Sloping to the Ocean

"Mendicants, the Yamuna river slants, slopes, and inclines to the ocean. …"

"… the Aciravatī river …"

"… the Sarabhu river …"

"… the Mahī river …"

"… all the great rivers …"

Pathamapacīnaninnasutta:

Slanting East

"Mendicants, the Ganges river slants, slopes, and inclines to the east.

In the same way, a mendicant who develops and cultivates the noble eightfold path slants, slopes, and inclines to extinguishment.

And how does a mendicant who develops the noble eightfold path slant, slope, and incline to extinguishment?

It's when a mendicant develops right view, right thought, right speech, right action, right livelihood, right effort, right mindfulness, and right immersion, which slants, slopes, and inclines to extinguishment.

That's how a mendicant who develops and cultivates the noble eightfold path slants, slopes, and inclines to extinguishment."

Dutiyadipacīnaninnasutta:

Slanting East

"Mendicants, the Yamuna river slants, slopes, and inclines to the east. …"

"… the Aciravatī river …"

"… the Sarabhu river …"

"… the Mahī river …"

"… all the great rivers …"

Pathamasamuddaninnasutta:

Slanting to the Ocean

"Mendicants, the Ganges river slants, slopes, and inclines to the ocean.

In the same way, a mendicant who develops and cultivates the noble eightfold path slants, slopes, and inclines to extinguishment.

And how does a mendicant who develops the noble eightfold path slant, slope, and incline to extinguishment?

It's when a mendicant develops right view, right thought, right speech, right action, right livelihood, right effort, right mindfulness, and right immersion, which slants, slopes, and inclines to extinguishment.

That's how a mendicant who develops and cultivates the noble eightfold path slants, slopes, and inclines to extinguishment."

Dutiyadisamuddaninnasutta:

Slanting to the Ocean

"Mendicants, the Yamuna river slants, slopes, and inclines to the ocean. ..."

"... the Aciravatī river ..."

"... the Sarabhu river ..."

"... the Mahī river ..."

"... all the great rivers ..."

Tathagatasutta:

The Realized One

At Savatthī.

"Mendicants, the Realized One, the perfected one, the fully awakened Buddha, is said to be the best of all sentient beings—be they footless, with two feet, four feet, or many feet; with form or formless; with perception or without perception or with neither perception nor non-perception.

In the same way, all skillful qualities are rooted in diligence and meet at diligence,

and diligence is said to be the best of them.

A mendicant who is diligent can expect to develop and cultivate the noble eightfold path.

And how does a mendicant who is diligent develop and cultivate the noble eightfold path?

It's when a mendicant develops right view, right thought, right speech, right action, right livelihood, right effort, right mindfulness, and right immersion, which rely on seclusion, fading away, and cessation, and ripen as letting go.

That's how a mendicant who is diligent develops and cultivates the noble eightfold path.

Mendicants, the Realized One, the perfected one, the fully awakened Buddha, is said to be the best of all sentient beings—be they footless, with two feet, four feet, or many feet; with form or formless; with perception or without perception or with neither perception nor non-perception.

In the same way, all skillful qualities are rooted in diligence and meet at diligence, and diligence is said to be the best of them.

A mendicant who is diligent can expect to develop and cultivate the noble eightfold path.

And how does a mendicant who is diligent develop and cultivate the noble eightfold path?

It's when a mendicant develops right view, right thought, right speech, right action, right livelihood, right effort, right mindfulness, and right immersion, which culminate in the removal of greed, hate, and delusion.

That's how a mendicant who is diligent develops and cultivates the noble eightfold path.

Mendicants, the Realized One, the perfected one, the fully awakened Buddha, is said to be the best of all sentient beings—be they footless, with two feet, four feet, or many feet; with form or formless; with perception or without perception or with neither perception nor non-perception.

In the same way, all skillful qualities are rooted in diligence and meet at diligence, and diligence is said to be the best of them.

A mendicant who is diligent can expect to develop and cultivate the noble eightfold path.

And how does a mendicant who is diligent develop and cultivate the noble eightfold path?

It's when a mendicant develops right view, right thought, right speech, right action, right livelihood, right effort, right mindfulness, and right immersion, which culminate, finish, and end in the deathless.

That's how a mendicant who is diligent develops and cultivates the noble eightfold path.

Mendicants, the Realized One, the perfected one, the fully awakened Buddha, is said to be the best of all sentient beings—be they footless, with two feet, four feet, or many feet; with form or formless; with perception or without perception or with neither perception nor non-perception.

In the same way, all skillful qualities are rooted in diligence and meet at diligence,

and diligence is said to be the best of them.

A mendicant who is diligent can expect to develop and cultivate the noble eightfold path.

And how does a mendicant who is diligent develop and cultivate the noble eightfold path?

It's when a mendicant develops right view, right thought, right speech, right action, right livelihood, right effort, right mindfulness, and right immersion, which slants, slopes, and inclines to extinguishment.

That's how a mendicant who is diligent develops and cultivates the noble eightfold path."

 Padasutta:

Footprints

"The footprints of all creatures that walk can fit inside an elephant's footprint.

So an elephant's footprint is said to be the biggest of them all.

In the same way, all skillful qualities are rooted in diligence and meet at diligence, and diligence is said to be the best of them.

A mendicant who is diligent can expect to develop and cultivate the noble eightfold path.

And how does a mendicant who is diligent develop and cultivate the noble eightfold path?

It's when a mendicant develops right view, right thought, right speech, right action, right livelihood, right effort, right mindfulness, and right immersion, which rely on seclusion, fading away, and cessation, and ripen as letting go. …

That's how a mendicant who is diligent develops and cultivates the noble eightfold path."

Kutadisutta:

A Roof Peak

"Mendicants, the rafters of a bungalow all lean to the peak, slope to the peak, and meet at the peak, so the peak is said to be the topmost of them all.

In the same way …"

(Tell in full as in the previous discourse.)

"Of all kinds of fragrant root, spikenard is said to be the best. …"

"Of all kinds of fragrant heartwood, red sandalwood is said to be the best. …"

"Of all kinds of fragrant flower, jasmine is said to be the best. …"

"All lesser kings are vassals of a wheel-turning monarch, so the wheel-turning monarch is said to be the foremost of them all. …"

Candimadisutta:

The Moon, Etc.

"The radiance of all the stars is not worth a sixteenth part of the moon's radiance, so the moon's radiance is said to be the best of them all. …"

"After the rainy season the sky is clear and cloudless. And when the sun rises, it dispels all the darkness from the sky as it shines and glows and radiates. …"

"Mendicants, cloth from Kasi is said to be the best kind of woven cloth. …"

(Tell these in full as in the section on the Realized One.)

 Balasutta:

Hard Work

At Savatthī.

"Mendicants, all the hard work that gets done depends on the earth and is grounded on the earth.

In the same way, a mendicant develops and cultivates the noble eightfold path depending on and grounded on ethics.

And how does a mendicant grounded on ethics develop and cultivate the noble eightfold path?

It's when a mendicant develops right view, right thought, right speech, right action, right livelihood, right effort, right mindfulness, and right immersion, which rely on seclusion, fading away, and cessation, and ripen as letting go.

That's how a mendicant grounded on ethics develops and cultivates the noble eightfold path."

"… which culminate in the removal of greed, hate, and delusion …"

"… culminate, finish, and end in the deathless …"

"… slants, slopes, and inclines to extinguishment …"

Bījasutta:

Seeds

"All the plants and seeds that achieve growth, increase, and maturity do so depending on the earth and grounded on the earth.

In the same way, a mendicant develops and cultivates the noble eightfold path depending on and grounded on ethics, achieving growth, increase, and maturity in good qualities.

And how does a mendicant develop the noble eightfold path depending on and grounded on ethics, achieving growth, increase, and maturity in good qualities?

It's when a mendicant develops right view, right thought, right speech, right action, right livelihood, right effort, right mindfulness, and right immersion, which rely on seclusion, fading away, and cessation, and ripen as letting go.

That's how a mendicant develops and cultivates the noble eightfold path depending on and grounded on ethics, achieving growth, increase, and maturity in good qualities."

Nagasutta:

Dragons

"Mendicants, dragons grow and wax strong supported by the Himalayas, the king of mountains.

When they're strong they dive into the pools. Then they dive into the lakes, the streams, the rivers, and finally the ocean. There they acquire a great and abundant body.

In the same way, a mendicant develops and cultivates the noble eightfold path depending on and grounded on ethics, acquiring great and abundant good qualities.

And how does a mendicant develop the noble eightfold path depending on and grounded on ethics, acquiring great and abundant good qualities?

It's when a mendicant develops right view, right thought, right speech, right action, right livelihood, right effort, right mindfulness, and right immersion, which rely on seclusion, fading away, and cessation, and ripen as letting go.

That's how a mendicant develops and cultivates the noble eightfold path depending on and grounded on ethics, acquiring great and abundant good qualities."

 Rukkhasutta:

Trees

"Mendicants, suppose a tree slants, slopes, and inclines to the east.

If it was cut off at the root, where would it fall?"

"Sir, it would fall in the direction that it slants, slopes, and inclines."

"In the same way, a mendicant who develops and cultivates the noble eightfold path slants, slopes, and inclines to extinguishment.

And how does a mendicant who develops the noble eightfold path slant, slope, and incline to extinguishment?

It's when a mendicant develops right view, right thought, right speech, right action, right livelihood, right effort, right mindfulness, and right immersion, which rely on seclusion, fading away, and cessation, and ripen as letting go.

That's how a mendicant who develops and cultivates the noble eightfold path slants, slopes, and inclines to extinguishment."

 Kumbhasutta:

Pots

"Mendicants, suppose a pot full of water is tipped over, so the water drains out and doesn't go back in.

In the same way, a mendicant who develops and cultivates the noble eightfold path expels bad, unskillful qualities and doesn't let them back in.

And how does a mendicant who develops the noble eightfold path expel bad, unskillful qualities and not let them back in?

It's when a mendicant develops right view, right thought, right speech, right action, right livelihood, right effort, right mindfulness, and right immersion, which rely on seclusion, fading away, and cessation, and ripen as letting go.

That's how a mendicant who develops and cultivates the noble eightfold path expels bad, unskillful qualities and doesn't let them back in."

Sukasutta:

A Spike

"Mendicants, suppose a spike of rice or barley was pointing the right way. If you trod on it with hand or foot, it may well break the skin and produce blood.

Why is that?

Because the spike is pointing the right way.

In the same way, a mendicant whose view and development of the path is pointing the right way may well break ignorance, produce knowledge, and realize extinguishment.

Why is that?

Because their view is pointing the right way.

And how does a mendicant whose view and development of the path is pointing the right way break ignorance, give rise to knowledge, and realize extinguishment?

It's when a mendicant develops right view, right thought, right speech, right action, right livelihood, right effort, right mindfulness, and right immersion, which rely on seclusion, fading away, and cessation, and ripen as letting go.

That's how a mendicant whose view and development of the path is pointing the right way breaks ignorance, gives rise to knowledge, and realizes extinguishment."

Akasasutta:

The Sky

"Mendicants, various winds blow in the sky.

Winds blow from the east, the west, the north, and the south. There are winds that are dusty and dustless, cool and warm, weak and strong.

In the same way, when the noble eightfold path is developed and cultivated the following are fully developed: the four kinds of mindfulness meditation, the four right efforts, the four bases of psychic power, the five faculties, the five powers, and the seven awakening factors.

And how are they fully developed?

It's when a mendicant develops right view, right thought, right speech, right action, right livelihood, right effort, right mindfulness, and right immersion, which rely on seclusion, fading away, and cessation, and ripen as letting go.

That's how they're fully developed."

Pathamamameghasutta:

Storms (1st)

"Mendicants, in the last month of summer, when the dust and dirt is stirred up, a large sudden storm disperses and settles it on the spot.

In the same way, a mendicant who develops and cultivates the noble eightfold path disperses and stills bad, unskillful qualities on the spot.

How does a mendicant who develops the noble eightfold path disperse and still bad, unskillful qualities on the spot?

It's when a mendicant develops right view, right thought, right speech, right action, right livelihood, right effort, right mindfulness, and right immersion, which rely on seclusion, fading away, and cessation, and ripen as letting go.

That's how a mendicant who develops and cultivates the noble eightfold path disperses and stills bad, unskillful qualities on the spot."

Dutiyameghasutta:

Storms (2nd)

"Mendicants, when a large storm has arisen, a strong wind disperses and settles it as it proceeds.

In the same way, a mendicant who develops and cultivates the noble eightfold path disperses and stills bad, unskillful qualities as they proceed.

And how does a mendicant who develops the noble eightfold path disperse and still bad, unskillful qualities as they proceed?

It's when a mendicant develops right view, right thought, right speech, right action, right livelihood, right effort, right mindfulness, and right immersion, which rely on seclusion, fading away, and cessation, and ripen as letting go.

That's how a mendicant who develops and cultivates the noble eightfold path disperses and stills bad, unskillful qualities as they proceed."

Navasutta:

A Ship

"Mendicants, suppose there was a sea-faring ship bound together with ropes. For six months they deteriorated in the water. Then in the cold season it was hauled up on dry land, where the ropes were weathered by wind and sun. When the clouds soaked it with rain, the ropes would readily collapse and rot away.

In the same way, when a mendicant develops and cultivates the noble eightfold path their fetters readily collapse and rot away.

And how do they develop and cultivate the noble eightfold path so that their fetters readily collapse and rot away?

It's when a mendicant develops right view, right thought, right speech, right action, right livelihood, right effort, right mindfulness, and right immersion, which rely on seclusion, fading away, and cessation, and ripen as letting go.

That's how they develop and cultivate the noble eightfold path so that their fetters readily collapse and rot away."

Agantukasutta:

A Guest House

"Mendicants, suppose there was a guest house. Lodgers come from the east, west, north, and south. Aristocrats, brahmins, merchants, and workers all stay there.

In the same way, a mendicant who develops and cultivates the noble eightfold path completely understands by direct knowledge the things that should be completely understood by direct knowledge.

They give up by direct knowledge the things that should be given up by direct knowledge. They realize by direct knowledge the things that should be realized by direct knowledge. They develop by direct knowledge the things that should be developed by direct knowledge.

And what are the things that should be completely understood by direct knowledge?

It should be said: the five grasping aggregates.

What five?

That is: form, feeling, perception, choices, and consciousness.

These are the things that should be completely understood by direct knowledge.

And what are the things that should be given up by direct knowledge?

Ignorance and craving for continued existence.

These are the things that should be given up by direct knowledge.

And what are the things that should be realized by direct knowledge?

Knowledge and freedom.

These are the things that should be realized by direct knowledge.

And what are the things that should be developed by direct knowledge?

Serenity and discernment.

These are the things that should be developed by direct knowledge.

And how does a mendicant develop the noble eightfold path in this way?

It's when a mendicant develops right view, right thought, right speech, right action, right livelihood, right effort, right mindfulness, and right immersion, which rely on seclusion, fading away, and cessation, and ripen as letting go.

That's how a mendicant develops and cultivates the eightfold path in this way."

Nadīsutta:

A River

"Mendicants, suppose that, although the Ganges river slants, slopes, and inclines to the east,

a large crowd were to come along with a spade and basket, saying:

'We'll make this Ganges river slant, slope, and incline to the west!'

What do you think, mendicants?

Would they succeed?"

"No, sir.

Why is that?

The Ganges river slants, slopes, and inclines to the east.

It's not easy to make it slant, slope, and incline to the west.

That large crowd will eventually get weary and frustrated."

"In the same way, while a mendicant develops and cultivates the noble eightfold path, if rulers or their ministers, friends or colleagues, relatives or family should invite them to accept wealth, saying:

'Please, mister, why let these ocher robes torment you?

Why follow the practice of shaving your head and carrying an alms bowl?

Come, return to a lesser life, enjoy wealth, and make merit!'

It's simply impossible for a mendicant who develops and cultivates the noble eightfold path to resign the training and return to a lesser life.

Why is that?

Because for a long time that mendicant's mind has slanted, sloped, and inclined to seclusion. So it's impossible for them to return to a lesser life.

And how does a mendicant develop the noble eightfold path?

It's when a mendicant develops right view, right thought, right speech, right action, right livelihood, right effort, right mindfulness, and right immersion, which rely on seclusion, fading away, and cessation, and ripen as letting go.

That's how a mendicant develops and cultivates the noble eightfold path."

 Esanasutta:

Searches

At Savatthī.

"Mendicants, there are these three searches.

What three?

The search for sensual pleasures, the search for continued existence, and the search for a spiritual path.

These are the three searches.

The noble eightfold path should be developed to directly know these three searches.

What is the noble eightfold path?

It's when a mendicant develops right view, right thought, right speech, right action, right livelihood, right effort, right mindfulness, and right immersion, which rely on seclusion, fading away, and cessation, and ripen as letting go.

This is the noble eightfold path that should be developed to directly know these three searches."

"Mendicants, there are these three searches.

What three?

The search for sensual pleasures, the search for continued existence, and the search for a spiritual path.

These are the three searches.

The noble eightfold path should be developed to directly know these three searches.

What is the noble eightfold path?

It's when a mendicant develops right view, right thought, right speech, right action, right livelihood, right effort, right mindfulness, and right immersion, which culminate in the removal of greed, hate, and delusion.

This is the noble eightfold path that should be developed to directly know these three searches."

"Mendicants, there are these three searches.

What three?

The search for sensual pleasures, the search for continued existence, and the search for a spiritual path.

These are the three searches.

The noble eightfold path should be developed to directly know these three searches.

What is the noble eightfold path?

It's when a mendicant develops right view, right thought, right speech, right action, right livelihood, right effort, right mindfulness, and right immersion, which culminate, finish, and end in the deathless.

This is the noble eightfold path that should be developed to directly know these three searches."

"Mendicants, there are these three searches.

What three?

The search for sensual pleasures, the search for continued existence, and the search for a spiritual path.

These are the three searches.

The noble eightfold path should be developed to directly know these three searches.

What is the noble eightfold path?

It's when a mendicant develops right view, right thought, right speech, right action, right livelihood, right effort, right mindfulness, and right immersion, which slants, slopes, and inclines to extinguishment.

This is the noble eightfold path that should be developed to directly know these three searches."

"Mendicants, there are these three searches.

What three?

The search for sensual pleasures, the search for continued existence, and the search for a spiritual path.

These are the three searches.

The noble eightfold path should be developed to completely understand …"

(Tell in full with "completely understand" instead of "directly know".)

"Mendicants, there are these three searches.

What three?

The search for sensual pleasures, the search for continued existence, and the search for a spiritual path.

These are the three searches.

The noble eightfold path should be developed to finish …"

(Tell in full with "finish" instead of "directly know".)

"Mendicants, there are these three searches.

What three?

The search for sensual pleasures, the search for continued existence, and the search for a spiritual path.

These are the three searches.

The noble eightfold path should be developed to give up …"

(Tell in full with "give up" instead of "directly know".)

Vidhasutta:

Discriminations

"Mendicants, there are three kinds of discrimination.

What three?

One discriminates, thinking that 'I'm better' or 'I'm equal' or 'I'm worse'.

These are the three kinds of discrimination.

The noble eightfold path should be developed for the direct knowledge, complete understanding, finishing, and giving up of these three kinds of discrimination.

What is the noble eightfold path?

It's when a mendicant develops right view, right thought, right speech, right action, right livelihood, right effort, right mindfulness, and right immersion, which rely on seclusion, fading away, and cessation, and ripen as letting go.

This is the noble eightfold path that should be developed for the direct knowledge, complete understanding, finishing, and giving up of these three kinds of discrimination."

(Tell in full as in the section on searches.)

Asavasutta:

Defilements

"Mendicants, there are these three defilements.

What three?

The defilements of sensuality, desire to be reborn, and ignorance.

These are the three defilements.

The noble eightfold path should be developed for the direct knowledge, complete understanding, finishing, and giving up of these three defilements."

Bhavasutta:

States of Existence

"There are these three states of existence.

What three?

Existence in the sensual realm, the realm of luminous form, and the formless realm.

These are the three states of existence.

The noble eightfold path should be developed for the direct knowledge, complete understanding, finishing, and giving up of these three states of existence."

Dukkhatasutta:

Forms of Suffering

"Mendicants, there are these three forms of suffering.

What three?

The suffering inherent in painful feeling; the suffering inherent in conditions; and the suffering inherent in perishing.

These are the three forms of suffering.

The noble eightfold path should be developed for the direct knowledge, complete understanding, finishing, and giving up of these three forms of suffering."

Khilasutta:

Kinds of Barrenness

"Mendicants, there are these three kinds of barrenness.

What three?

Greed, hate, and delusion.

These are the three kinds of barrenness.

The noble eightfold path should be developed for the direct knowledge, complete understanding, finishing, and giving up of these three kinds of barrenness."

 Malasutta:

Stains

"Mendicants, there are these three stains.

What three?

Greed, hate, and delusion.

These are the three stains.

The noble eightfold path should be developed for the direct knowledge, complete understanding, finishing, and giving up of these three stains."

 Nīghasutta:

Troubles

"Mendicants, there are these three troubles.

What three?

Greed, hate, and delusion.

These are the three troubles.

The noble eightfold path should be developed for the direct knowledge, complete understanding, finishing, and giving up of these three troubles."

Vedanasutta:

Feelings

"Mendicants, there are these three feelings:

What three?

Pleasant, painful, and neutral feeling.

These are the three feelings.

The noble eightfold path should be developed for the direct knowledge, complete understanding, finishing, and giving up of these three feelings."

Tanhasutta:

Craving

"Mendicants, there are these three cravings.

What three?

Craving for sensual pleasures, craving to continue existence, and craving to end existence.

These are the three cravings.

The noble eightfold path should be developed for the direct knowledge, complete understanding, finishing, and giving up of these three cravings.

What is the noble eightfold path?

It's when a mendicant develops right view, right thought, right speech, right action, right livelihood, right effort, right mindfulness, and right immersion, which rely on seclusion, fading away, and cessation, and ripen as letting go.

This is the noble eightfold path that should be developed for the direct knowledge, complete understanding, finishing, and giving up of these three cravings."

Tasinasutta

Thirst

"Mendicants, there are these three thirsts.

What three?

Thirst for sensual pleasures, thirst to continue existence, and thirst to end existence.

For the direct knowledge, complete understanding, finishing, and giving up of these three thirsts …

… which culminates in the removal of greed, hate, and delusion.

… which culminates, finishes, and ends in the deathless.

… which slants, slopes, and inclines to extinguishment.

The noble eightfold path should be developed for the direct knowledge, complete understanding, finishing, and giving up of these three thirsts."

Oghasutta:

Floods

At Savatthī.

"Mendicants, there are these four floods.

What four?

The floods of sensuality, desire to be reborn, views, and ignorance.

These are the four floods.

The noble eightfold path should be developed for the direct knowledge, complete understanding, finishing, and giving up of these four floods."

(Tell in full as in the section on searches.)

Yogasutta:

Attachments

"Mendicants, there are these four attachments.

What four?

The attachment to sensual pleasures, future lives, views, and ignorance.

These are the four attachments.

The noble eightfold path should be developed for the direct knowledge, complete understanding, finishing, and giving up of these four attachments."

Upadanasutta:

Grasping

"Mendicants, there are these four kinds of grasping.

What four?

Grasping at sensual pleasures, views, precepts and observances, and theories of a self.

These are the four kinds of grasping.

The noble eightfold path should be developed for the direct knowledge, complete understanding, finishing, and giving up of these four kinds of grasping."

Ganthasutta:

Personal Ties

"Mendicants, there are these four ties.

What four?

The personal ties to covetousness, ill will, misapprehension of precepts and observances, and the insistence that this is the only truth.

These are the four ties.

The noble eightfold path should be developed for the direct knowledge, complete understanding, finishing, and giving up of these four ties."

Anusayasutta:

Tendencies

"Mendicants, there are these seven underlying tendencies.

What seven?

The underlying tendencies of sensual desire, repulsion, views, doubt, conceit, desire to be reborn, and ignorance.

These are the seven underlying tendencies.

The noble eightfold path should be developed for the direct knowledge, complete understanding, finishing, and giving up of these seven underlying tendencies."

Kamagunasutta:

Kinds of Sensual Stimulation

"Mendicants, there are these five kinds of sensual stimulation.

What five?

Sights known by the eye that are likable, desirable, agreeable, pleasant, sensual, and arousing.

Sounds known by the ear ... Smells known by the nose ...

Tastes known by the tongue ...

Touches known by the body that are likable, desirable, agreeable, pleasant, sensual, and arousing.

These are the five kinds of sensual stimulation.

The noble eightfold path should be developed for the direct knowledge, complete understanding, finishing, and giving up of these five kinds of sensual stimulation."

Nīvaranasutta:

Hindrances

"Mendicants, there are these five hindrances.

What five?

The hindrances of sensual desire, ill will, dullness and drowsiness, restlessness and remorse, and doubt.

These are the five hindrances.

The noble eightfold path should be developed for the direct knowledge, complete understanding, finishing, and giving up of these five hindrances."

Upadanakkhandhasutta:

Grasping Aggregates

"Mendicants, there are these five grasping aggregates.

What five?

The grasping aggregates of form, feeling, perception, choices, and consciousness.

These are the five grasping aggregates.

The noble eightfold path should be developed for the direct knowledge, complete understanding, finishing, and giving up of these five grasping aggregates."

Orambhagiyasutta:

Lower Fetters

"Mendicants, there are five lower fetters.

What five?

Identity view, doubt, misapprehension of precepts and observances, sensual desire, and ill will.

These are the five lower fetters.

The noble eightfold path should be developed for the direct knowledge, complete understanding, finishing, and giving up of these five lowers fetters."

Uddhambhagiyasutta:

Higher Fetters

"Mendicants, there are five higher fetters.

What five?

Desire for rebirth in the realm of luminous form, desire for rebirth in the formless realm, conceit, restlessness, and ignorance.

These are the five higher fetters.

The noble eightfold path should be developed for the direct knowledge, complete understanding, finishing, and giving up of these five higher fetters.

What is the noble eightfold path?

It's when a mendicant develops right view, right thought, right speech, right action, right livelihood, right effort, right mindfulness, and right immersion, which rely on seclusion, fading away, and cessation, and ripen as letting go.

This is the noble eightfold path that should be developed for the direct knowledge, complete understanding, finishing, and giving up of these five higher fetters."

"Mendicants, there are five higher fetters.

What five?

Desire for rebirth in the realm of luminous form, desire for rebirth in the formless realm, conceit, restlessness, and ignorance.

These are the five higher fetters.

The noble eightfold path should be developed for the direct knowledge, complete understanding, finishing, and giving up of these five higher fetters.

What is the noble eightfold path?

It's when a mendicant develops right view, right thought, right speech, right action, right livelihood, right effort, right mindfulness, and right immersion, which culminate in the removal of greed, hate, and delusion …"

"… which culminate, finish, and end in the deathless …"

"… which slant, slope, and incline to extinguishment.

This is the noble eightfold path that should be developed for the direct knowledge, complete understanding, finishing, and giving up of these five higher fetters."